# Tidal Interlude

Gopal Lahiri

**SHAMBHABI**
The Third Eye Imprint

1

Published by: Prabir Roy at **Shambhabi – The Third Eye Imprint**, A-10/1, Amarabati, Sodepur, Kolkata 700110

1st edition (India): December, 2015

Global Distributor: Shambhabi – The Third Eye Imprint



Cover design: Prabir Roy & Bitan Chakraborty

ISBN-13: 978-81-931666-7-3 [Paperback]



Price: INR Two hundred and fifty only [Rs.250/- only]

Dedicated to


Kiriti Sengupta

&

Prabir Roy

*... It's difficult to speak but impossible to be silent*

# Mapping The Wilderness Of The Mind

Poetry is the spontaneous overflow of powerful feelings: it takes its origin from emotion recollected in tranquillity — William Wordsworth

Gopal Lahiri's current poetry collection, Tidal Interlude certainly conforms to Wordsworth's renowned definition of poetry. There is emotion here and amidst tranquil interludes, there is a powerful and spontaneous tide of feelings.

This collection is a journey into solitude; into the poet's mindscape, profound, philosophic, yet not totally unrealistic. Many of the poems are snatched moments of time, spun into unhurried music, meditating on man, nature and fragments of cityscape - flitting effortlessly in and out of each stratum is the poetic sensibility. Tidal Interlude sums up a certain musical quality that is echoed in the fine verse that reminds one of "dewy silence(s) and clear crisp twilight of big skies and empty landscapes." These poems are the reflections of an accomplished poet, who weaves a beautiful web of temporal spaces in contrasting shades of light and darkness.

The poems highlight *panchabhuta* or the five elements of Indian philosophy and aesthetic: earth, water, air, fire and sky. The collection is a tapestry, each poem poising on its own and also rolling out in a close-knit intrinsic pattern. Subtle metaphors and refined sensory images sketch the terrains of the poet's mindscape and his perception of the outside world, knitting an exquisite arabesque of the inner and outer self. Lahiri's is a distinct elemental voice mapping the wilderness of the mind.

There is an elegance in Lahiri's verse that highlights intricate craftsmanship: in the linear arrangement, in the syntactical inventiveness and in the exquisite literary devices that wing around like birds in flight. The recurrent motif of birds voices the poet's thoughts that read the unknown in the colours of the rainbow. Birds assume the role of metaphysical conceits, while simultaneously carrying out their flights and birdsong, while being "tossed in the blue sky." The poetic persona is a "solitary bird making rounds in a way of finding the art of survival", providing occasional wing-flashes of autobiographical feathers.

However, this tranquil collection has vibrant tracts of resistance: in allusions to injustice, in references to past pain, in attempts to break walls of silence and glass doors. The shift in emphasis from philosophic reflection to rebellious angst is dramatic: Now my hands are chopped, my skin is burnt, my face is blackened /Do not wash me in holy water/ I cannot join in your prayer in the temple. This "melancholy strain" on "natural sorrow, loss or pain" is cyclical throughout the collection and certainly takes you by surprise at every corner.

I have read and re-read the poems; each new reading unveiling tiers of new meaning. I bear the verses in my mind, long after the lines have vanished from my eyes.

Usha Kishore

Poet and Translator
Isle of Man
October, 2015

# Language As Poetics

*The creative universe of Gopal Lahiri*

With Gopal Lahiri, you hear each word speak clearly! The Mumbai-based earth-scientist is very sharp when it comes to crafting a tech report for the specialists or a sparkling poem for the connoisseurs. And each word counts in the composition: The dewy silence, clear crisp twilight, big skies and empty landscapes — well, the words deployed are so every day and simple but undergo a quick metamorphosis in the poetic hands of Gopal and assume a special property called by consensus as lyrical! Only talented poets possess this quality that makes their compositions so outstanding.

Lahiri's fans already know and swear on oath to the outside world — his genius as an acute observer of the usual, the ordinary, the everyday and aestheticizing those tiny bits and fragments into startling metaphors and images and words that glow like the *jugnoo* or fireflies in the scented dark of a verdant valley. Gopal brings an extra edge to the lived experience in spaces urban; wild; touristy or solitary. Everything is under his probing gaze and ideas and images combine in a strange alchemy and become texts of intense luminosity and density! It is heavy stuff occasionally but ultimately, the poet is able to convey with all clarity the surge of competing ideas in a masterly way to his intended audiences

The present collection of his poems opens up linguistic and imagistic wonderland where each item — a vigorous wind or a tender twig or a wandering star — is catalogued with precision and talk to you, like each element in a Picasso mosaic.

Here is a book that you will long cherish for its inherent artistic delights, post-reading — like the digital take-home pictures of a happy family vacation for their time-defying, spectral value.

Sunil Sharma

Poet, Critic and Writer
November, 2015
Maharashtra, India

# Introduction

"Do people still read poetry?" This question revolves around for a while to me and this also alarmingly suggests: "Poets are only talking to each other."

In doing so, somewhere along the way, the overreaching impulse behind the writing poems has been dwindling over the years. It is also true that very few people read contemporary poetry but still poetry survives ages and highlights some key moments and trajectories of life. "The heightened consciousness" in poetry still reminds us that the ideas are not necessarily doomed in "utopia and dreamscape."

It's every poets dream to be read, to be recognized for lifting the submerged soul and casting light into the dark corner of the life. "Poetry makes nothing happen" wrote Auden but it is also true that poetry can offer ways of understanding the present and it's relation with the past. It can be argued that poetry has retained its power even now and is a stress buster in corporate jargon as well as a weapon in troubled times.

*Tidal Interlude* is my third poetry collection after *Silent Steps* and *Living Inside*. Readers may like to know why "Tidal Interlude?" Admittedly, nature has a special place in my poems and tide is a recurring motif which reflects energy of swell and the inherent interlude.

We know, "Poetry is the place where language performs." The celebrations of the enduring human values during the journey from "abstract to concrete," the "eternal spirit" as Byron wrote and the mother nature appeal to me which go to leave the noise of the world behind and hopefully reconnect with the mosaic of words in my poems.

Like in my earlier collections, I wish that after reading my poetry, the readers will walk away with a sense of the life and history, its beauty and its relevance. I do hope in the end that above all, my readers will take pleasure in reading the poems in *Tidal Interlude*.

Gopal Lahiri

December, 2015
Mumbai, India

# Acknowledgements

I am indebted to Usha Kishore for her in-depth evaluation of my poems in *Tidal Interlude*. She is a poet per excellence and her thoughts are always an inspiration to me.

Dr Sunil Sharma is a warm advocate for poetry and is instrumental in encouraging me to write poems better. My sincere thanks to him for his luminous words of creative universe and feeling in my poems.

I am also thankful to the well-known poets, Rob Harle, David J Delaney and Gary Robinson for their wonderful analysis and feedback for my poems in 'Tidal Interlude'.

I extend my sincere thanks to the eminent poets, Vihang Naik, Jaydeep Sarangi, Prabhanjan K. Mishra and Seshu Chamarty for their blessings and kind words on my poems.

I am grateful to the talented poet and writer Dr Kiriti Sengupta and Prabir Roy for their support and counsel and for enjoying the task of converting the digital words into the printed pages.

Finally, I also receive welcome advice from my dear friends and fellow poets as well as readers. To all, my thanks.

# Contents

# Secret Code

for now though,
the optimum happiness signatures are those
in the eyes of the rain washed birds
tempered with silken feathers and rummaged greenery,

the austerity of décor in the evening colors
reminds of a moment that time forgot,
of dewy silence and clear crisp twilight
of big skies and empty landscapes,

along a narrow path
the birds tossed in the blue sky
that marked out in *Shimul* branches,

stepping inside
falling in the dark whirl,

the secret code that reopens
the wooden door to freedom,
for now the earth is at peace,

soothed by the steady breeze, the distant calls fade in
there will be worship in the temples
in the times of deepest peace
that ends with calmness and tears of joy.

# Window

sitting alone, searching for that rare connection,
look furtively into the window with rusted grills,
the sunrays shifting against the constricted deadlines,
seeking space and a distinct range of reference,
finally settle with the advent of smoky clouds.

interrupted by allusions of unwanted darkness
a gust of wind that is unmatched in its vigor,
seems to work, sync with time, at least somewhat,
the evening requires perhaps an accurate face-time,
with the fragmented text and a quirky set of notes.

one can spot a strategy on every limb of the township
the rain drenched grass grown over the rocky surface,
the seed germinates, enjoying diplomatic immunity,
still there, sitting on the rough edges, fight for survival
the way they fall only to reach the ground for support.

a tall tree haunted by the shades of dead leaves,
making no attempt to camouflage true feelings,
still needs powerful leg-up to view that lies beyond,
the painted four walls coldly disown the filtered
light through the series of uneven wooden shutters,

"there's a thought" though, holding hands with
the one you always share precious moments.
that explodes and perishes long ago into ashes,
yet striving to keep alive reward or laconic rudeness
to show the balanced view from the other side.

# Debate

a simmering debate that rages daily,
hiding away inside the cocoon,
slowly fades away
in the growing bustle.

this stained glass window
overlooking the misty peaks,
is perhaps the perfect pod
in the dark chilly evening.

keys, bank cards, cigarette packets
and a set of notes are on the table,
now all those wooden chairs
do not have any right of opinion.

all pervading silence in its purest form
shines in the four blank wall.
The burning eyes peeled though,
rarely provide the answers.

if all this is true and it may well be
then holding the hidden words
under the shadowy light
in the crucified morning hue
may not reveal the real story.

# Water

An earthen lamp floats on the serene meandering river.
Flickering of light raises hope, emits trust, and spells
truth.

The ripples sound low, unstated for a while.
Bleary evening settles quietly on the river water.

The fading colour of the twilight pushes the envelope.
Of the starry night and the whispering breeze.

The ringing sound of the distant temple bell,
A link between the past and the primordial,

Losing altitude the birds wind up their songs all too
quickly.
A life lived with flaws, a drawing on a broader palette,

That stifles youth, innovation and that of planting seeds
Unable to infuse essentials to make failure a success.

Twenty steps to go down, the inviting music of freedom
A tortuous path travelled in anguish and misery,

Can a light from within spark and shine in darkness?
Touch the cold water, a way forward to sink and touch

Washing the dirt and sin, change the way others look at...
The river bed, the ultimate refuge to lie down and rest
forever.

# Time Warp

Months ago we discussed about
What was or what could have been lost,
withdrawn and terse,
you did not lift your sunken eyes.

gone were the empty sockets, but
the spirit-lamp was there,
stuck in a time warp,
turning darkness into light, light into haze.

The shadows behaved like the
intolerant bullies, nothing to do with grief,
We saw it but did not flinch,
and only clipped the unknown voices.

Vermillion in a glass case
shaped and revised memories,
behind the steel mirror,
The broken words left unsaid.

looking at the night birds in flight
searching for something,
we debated for long hours
and the raging fire burnt all night.

# Prayer

I may be infant, baby, teenager, grown up, adult
do not give me any name
I want to be nameless.

Do not make me a loving pet
to get your work done.

I am not aware when you throw fireball
when you fight, pounce, tear apart,
put me in a prison.

Your eyes never told me the truth.

You never know my hands are rivers
far away in the hill,
I love to watch sky
in silence,
I speak galaxy.

But you never listen to me

Now my hands are chopped, my skin is burnt, my face is
blackened.

Do not wash me in holy water.

I cannot join in your prayer in the temple.

# Dream

Remember that sun in last summer!
mellowed and withdrawn,

looking through the curtain of the window,
something so tender about it,
simple like moving pages after pages,

yet in my imagined voyage of discovery,
I hammer the nail to fix in the wall
amidst the unsettling shade of green,

and the resistance towards it,
near the kitchen table, the cracks are
now swiftly disposed of.

no languor here,
no words can be leaked
through the soft palm,

a house is full of shadows, crawling,
silence is an old wound that
will open the wooden door,

what we talk about,
nothing has happened really,
in my sleep light plays beautifully,
still I feel so close, I dream about it.

so many ways of looking,
all those mounds crumble,
let my dreams move in silence.

## Glass Door


Sailing, skimming, tuning its strings
The white clouds,
Wheels clatter on outside,
Just as dangerous as when I was a child.

The glass door separates us- the cycle bells,
Memories of the thumbnail reflections,
Faintly remind the tender touches,
For washing away the tears, the watery cheek.

Drawing the white lace curtains
I look at it again,
Then with sidelong glance,
That allows my escape.

The paper balls hidden inside a drawer
Now lying open in my palm,
Just as light as tufts of feathers,
I begin here.

The murky room clawing with sharp knives
Covering a multitude of sins,
Is guilty of having
Nothing to declare.

Rummaging through the torn papers,
Trashing stories that do not wear out,
I can glimpse  your fingers reach out
And cut the knots of the umbilical chord

# Breaking Wall

there is a gentleness in the morning sky.
you open the door, smile back at the sparse clouds
it's now much easier
to forget the dark dreams.

time to get to know one another over a cup of tea,
a surge of inner life, a sense of empowerment, alive still,
even the woolen blankets
retain the delicate crease.

now the wooden backrest resists your probing fingers,
but you don't know the memory of the hidden scars.
saying grimly
'we are not ourselves any more'.

you love to stand above in the plateau of flowers
try to reach the razing sun and burn in flames,
be there so long to fill
the earth with raining ashes,

there is only one departure in your direction
you remember what it means, breaking the wall
inside, you stand
desolate, frozen in the icy wind.

# Admission

Now that it has begun
As though in a time of deepest harmony.

In a circle of sound,
There was a faint flush of tears

How painful it was in the past-
The footsteps missing the altitude in staircases.

On one level, the unerring truth
of sharp knife pressed in,
and the stain erased in a breathing world.

Yet far behind the blank wall
Someone did dredge up memories,
Ashen and grotesque.

Looking at the glass window
the fragile bones of the lonely comet could
easily fall and spill.

The starry night
Silent and still,
Burdened with mystery and milky ways,

Told more than you could tell.

# My Space

Between the light and the shade
Air is thickened with dust,
You know, too far has gone,
Yet, critics slam non-existent crisis.

For now, I am happy in my closet
Knowing that the evening breeze will
Refill the minnows; dry leaves
Blown away, petals fall in a hurry.

Stay behind on the earthy wasteland,
You mean to live life harder, and yet,
In order to escape the despair and grief,
Shade them with your softest palm.

Look up at the cloudless sky
I believe it in all, barely understand,
Facing the blank stonewall and cry
Again the moon comes in and out,

The darkness beating to the tune of
Silence, wrestles with the trials,
A deep dive in space and resolve
like a simple and short equation.

# That Is Unknown

Perhaps, it's only slip, not fall, in search of hidden pole
The paper trails, the unread notes, the empty desk,

Candles dot the tables; light and luminescence
Low lit chandeliers flirting with the moonshine outside.

Seeing through discordant space that was derelict
Blur the distinction, as if transfixed, amorous,

Human touch that makes it big; cementing ties,
Seen through my window; Long hike through lush hills,

Look closely and it's up there in the darkness,
Who is around us, teaches us something about time wrap.

Emerging a figure; that is unknown even in fire and
fester.
A nebulous line, ferocious and brutal to destroy us.

Nothing of that sorts happen...What is over is over,
A torn diary full of sadness, drops down into dust.

Let go the past and move on. The wall clock reminds...
Entice the sky to come down to this beautiful earth.

# Undone

Two layers of meaning; your note on the diary,
Kept on the old wooden desk;
unattended.

Seen the torn pages flutter in the breeze,
Things you could have
written long before.

Did you travel too fast? Did you darken your thoughts?
Something has already gone back to the cradle,
beyond your reach.

There was a visible labour, an attempt to survive,
But the light was always dim, a long decline
shadows lengthened.

The boats were languishing on the riverside
Turned slowly, waiting for the high tide
Roamed like flies and insects
The unknown promises.

You tried, pushed yourself to the life; bright and burning
Not cried over for the loss,
not allowed to flow from your eyes.

I knew you missed that sailing boat,
All was not well – your eyes told
Renewal, rebirth turning to grimace.

# Fire Within

in the space between
the iron grill and leafy branches
separates and unites-
a day passes,
I see the sky spreading
far from the green earth.

to trap the unchecked sunlight
in my glass jar
I close my eyes and
take a deep breath
and light up the fire

the color I see is red
these days no one step down
to tell when I'm ready,
clobber and whack me
to put my finger on.

still you lead me
through a narrow passage
leading the fire wall
into the shape of an eye
reading rainbow's color.

# Uneven Path

the solitary bird making rounds
in a way of finding,
the art of survival on
uneven paths and graft,
keeping it buried,
softness sets in the twilight sun.

milky white cloud flakes
high and low of the window breeze,
life to be in a half or full circle
world in a microcosm,
seal the glorious moments.
painfully evoke sensation

no one seems to care that
sea gulls wheeling over the
vast expanse of blue water,
beach cafes keen with locals
dense stands of coconut palms
always care for geometry.

When our heart beats
There will be silence,
walking on the diagonals
the hanging question
closes in opposites.

# Claw Back

the curtain rips open,
the stone wall collapses,
all those who hurry over
to snatch the golden rabbit
slowly disappear.

And through the hole
light flickering
in the dark alley
infuses life
brings a new trajectory
to the inky sky.

.

the street dogs
take the voice
as their weapons;
the strong wind deletes
the archaic code of the silence.

for years suffocated, mutilated,
the resolution is for taking hold,
they raise their voices,
increase the decibel,
gaining firm ground.

ideas melt in the heart,
burn inside, set the tone
protest gaining momentum,
they light the candle,
hit the emptiness and walk along.

# Diary

a few round words, a deliberate gap,
then the fragments of other texts,
flip into the pages,
there the stains of ink,
the rhythms and the play of words gone,
crawling shadows can't rest on their laurels,
surprised that you like fleeting images.

finding that name so many times
doesn't truly lives into the present,
interrupted by
a few dots and squiggles,
the bird with frosted wings cry,
a repository of names and names only,
the responses never shift really
losing the biting wit and clarity.

enraged that the diary still riffs on
the winnowing past as the endpoint,
the fight between the spine and scalpel,
a spectacle that
well worth observing,
pages can never store the cumulated tears
like disparate disorganized raindrops,
something feels misplaced and scrambled.

# Unscripted Moments

Let the candle burn
For the flame for the shadow on the wall.
outside world turns real.
It's a long rainy moments brings back to the world
a low sound over the window-
Moist Glass drips rain water, on the site of loss
The soft echoes and vibrations not just sitting in them,
Asking for more darkness, interlocked with the
surroundings-
Mother and daughter share the secrets now
Of life and beyond. The raging lines haunt each other,
stretching to a break point,
Of violence, abuse and resign, of table-ware and shattered
glass, mirror, all the mire against the dark,
Of dust and grime, carpets and cushions,
Set of their shoulders, then with the tilt of their heads
Plowing through the drift of words, squirming under the
lights,
Nearly buried beneath their skins.
you are only the silent witness recoiling the unscripted
moments,
drop poison in the folded hands.

# The Wall Of Silence

Scrubbed its walls, deconstructed,
people can slip through the cracks;
escape with only sadness.

a stack of six burnt chapattis,
roofs scorching black
from the cooking fire,

empty sacks of flour
filthy water in a mug, cold,
at the edge of the garbage dump.

a squinty eyed rickety woman
scratching her old wounds,
numbed, scarred.

stick to her side
bloated bellies, blank faces of children,
sucking their thumbs.
lives continues to be lived.

pungent smoke fills the dirty lanes,
the silver moon besieged,
melts slowly in despair.
songs continue to be sung in silence.

# Little Light

In this courtyard
I can play with the vanishing blue.
it is all but eloquent silence.
I can be summer, words melt,
when I see the clouds splitting blood,
the leaves rustle in despair,
drop me weightless, motionless.
I can be sunrise with memories,
in this open space, away from the valley.
even when rain soaks the wrinkled skin
I can hear the perfect pitch-
out for a tryst,.
when I sing a song for you
a little light washes my face,
Until the sun slips behind the brick wall,
there are more treats,
Going inside to greet you
I feel a sense of coming home.
When the wind surrenders to the trampled grass
I remember my mother
washes me in cold water.

# Down Under

we started in silence stared
all around us,
her face was an eerie beauty
in suffering,
by the sun's glare,
by whipping rain,

whack, heave, hammer
the violent words
fell secretly remorseless,
glowed with the sadness,
floating somewhere inside
succumbed to the sound
of her voice.

finding refuge in eyes
of the unfulfilled,
might not be
all that longer
the late evening shadows
down under.

her face became
calm and steel,
smite, scythe, clobber
the setting sun.
took a sleep out of me.

I wake up in midnight
that was yesterday.

# Kernels

Sometimes words are torn polythene bag
deflowered by pain and wounds.

the forest have shrunk
the wise men once played a vital role but
they are less human now.

the birds and bees are in uncertain future
animal skeletons lay bare, dusted leaves,
who can be our best allies?

Sometimes words are bold and luminous
bring fish bones and charcoal night.

We're told- the furnace faces push the barriers
the grey morning rustles in silence.

the attacks withstood, care for nothing else,
of escaping from the long suffering.

Sometimes words are secret seeds
they bring new metaphors for life.
they do this day in and day out.

# Tide # Wallflower

From between the fire and wood
I will reach for ashes,
The twilight clouds like rosary sausage
End up in
Pulping evening stories.

Because it makes sense
The merrymakers play with rippled beds
Sharing thoughts,
Stride down to the tidal inlets.

The low mounds crumble
In this marshy land,
And that path they take
Feel the cracking.

The ambushed birds
Making rounds overhead,
Cannot understand the errors
In wind direction.

I script the footprints but missing lines,
That drags me backwards
And then I know the gentle push
Of the sheared wallflower.

# Shadow

Searching for something...

Leave me in the lurch
my shadows act of intolerance
And intimidation percolate
through the stretches of soft words
And ignoble lyrics
Deeper into my soul.

It does not matter
If I become immobile
In frozen silence,
Yet the Old horses of the derelict temple
Withdrawn and pithy,
Hard to pin down the reality,

They remain there for years.
Knowing what it is to live,
I will not allow my shadow to do violence,
continue protest with scruffy muscles and limbs
Until it ceases,
Erases the chalk line dark with muck
And stand tall amidst ruins.

# Desolate Ghat

Standing on the edges of the slippery
Steps of the desolate ghat,
I count the minutes in my palm,
The setting sun plummets slowly
Over the river Hooghly

The old magic of the sliced moon
Cold, sensual, pale,
reading lips- not known,
Join the tributaries, coalesce and
Floating downwards
Under a bold night sky.

The hushed presence of danger
Too fine, too balanced
Lying open,

The darkness has tamed
The female night birds
Converse in a male voice,

For a landscape skewed by time
The aroma wafted by the cool breeze,
Ebb and flow of the water,
Voices settle on the stony path.

In spite of everything, the wheeze
the slender and slim,
Trees making songs,
till night's dark maze
dissolves in the rising sun.

# Exit Route

Hidden in you, a kernel, a spark, so unique,
Guru says, the secret of the seed- it's about
Learning to trust your strength
Wrapped in everyday chaos and cauldron.

Grin shades into a mischievous smirk
Nursing a snarling and recurring cough
Helpless as I am always,
Numbed, scraped, wounded inside.

You can add in moments of yellow light
Filter through an open window,
Sips my dreams, melts in desire yet
Strikes the false notes in dots and ellipses.

Doesn't finish there, for something
Fake and forged, brutal and graphic
Doing sketches of the dark comedy
Less helpful, I feel like taking exit route.

# Flame Tree

Flame tree petal I like,
Pinnate with petiole,
The dry leaves
And the pod like fruits.

Under the red hot sun,
Layers of orange-red flame
In its full bloom in this parched land.

The large cracks in
your wind-weathered face,
map a distant lonely path.

Like your blood stained hand
Recalls dusty wind, fallen leaflets,
Take a bite of you,
Absorb the strong scent of deer musk.

I dream I am awake, gazing at a
Willowy knife
with sharp blade
and the chill of too much red hues.

Pressing my forehead against the
Flame of the forest
A brush of dry skin,
Waiting for shining nails of your love.

# Inner Circle

Looking through the shining mirrored wall,
seeking inner space,
distinct warmth in eyes,
wonder and elation lithely going dark,
slender, curved, piercing moon burns inside.

one voice whispers, the other one muted,
a sense of being haunted by the shadow.
the leafy trees as proud as they can be
words and bones complement each other.

a meeting that's really hard to imagine
Orion belt and its shoulder,
empty stars feel as real,
a narrow territory between love and light
the anguished mind always drives into tears.

becomes visible in inner circle, behind eyes.
for when all is said, the question of the
existence of you and me in this vast universe,
a force infusing, the flow moves in torrents.

unfold in all directions the rows of small
stone houses dotted
with engraved faces,
point towards the eastern wavy shoreline
of being there, in search of the second path.

dreams and meaning of the balanced life
flicker through, survives and thrives here.
in a way to accept the celebrations of dawn
the music of the universe rings in delight.

## Muted Color


Some days, in my village, rain
comes with dirt
a pool of water, slippery steps
on the courtyard.
thatched leaking roof, it's easy to remember
the day, in the darkness too.
that we are promised
to weave dreams, smell of the wet soil, those
leaning bushes
on the bamboo fence reveal
a heavy shower with strong winds.


the distant
rolling voice and then a veil of silence.
the jackfruit tree on the courtyard clutching
low hanging fruits,


poisonous snakes between
the two wind-warped guava groves, a sigh
of relief, looming over this, in the darkness,


the ghost who do not have the ability to catch
the light, everything falls away
at the wayside.


the long held secret code
to unlock the wooden door, but the clay wall collapses,
and in word,


we cannot explain
the hidden lines. no space now to hold your wrinkled
face,
my mother earth.

# Ink And Paper

I know what ink and paper is all about,
tears of despair in eyes
and erosion of values.
it never says about the
tide and wallflower.

but the time is stuck in reverse here
back across the mango tree,
outside on the courtyard, the
clay mound crumbles
and drops down to dirt.

from the wooden door to the garden
was once a long walk,
between the two rows of palm trees
tune to the bells
of the Kali temple.

the evening often speaks soft words
of the black oriole,
and still makes sense, that path
we travel, never think of
so many near misses.

Today it's just an image
goes in and out of the clouds
under the pale moon,
Remembering
our meandering thoughts.

# Fort Kochi

The Chinese fishing nets abound here
suspend horizontally over the sea,
bamboo poles,
the rising wind reminds long history
in the flaps and whistles
of the white sea birds,

In your thoughts, going against
the comfort of sitting idle,
the images that left behind,
of the coconut trees
reclaims identity in delicate pastels,
against the setting sun,

the carved faces of the distant island,
evening wakes up
with mugs of coffee
tall and short people drink unmindfully
smell and taste memory,
weaving and spilling short stories,

ebbing of the light, darkening of the sky
how well we heeded
the evening words,
of the time capsule relic,
how far we have advanced
in tremulous cadences.

click on the billowing clouds,
every moment is changing and different.
eventually the forceful whispers,
reveal the power of argument.
The singe of the soul in the fading light.

# Battle

On one of those days
I can lay hands in the charcoal fire
Dip them and dig deep down
Imagine a battle inside,

On nothing but a malachite green field,
I can catch a butterfly in a faded evening
On the overflowing banks,

Carry over the river
Your voice runs my head,
I don't know when-

Shadows never beat in summer
My veins are my tributaries
They flow and change path,

Dance in ecstasy,
Beaten by the rocks, pebbles and
The iron hand,
Of work half-done.

The bunch of green leaves, Mobil oil,
Dirt and plastics
Of whites roses and ribbons,
Stepping down from the soaring cliffs
The life that steals oxygen

We can borrow time-
I know only this song.

# Eternal Love

There will be evening strolls soon,
the fallen leaves gently
recoiling form the memory.
if I need green, it needs to go down inside.

Let your hair drifts away,
the strong wind pushes
them towards my face,
your eyes recording notes of the summer evening.

I press my forehead
with your delicate fingers
it's soft, intimate,
close my eyes, smell the fragrance
tracing the curve, of your full lips.

A second or a minute or an hour
passes by in silence, we plead,
Do not shout for joy,
Do not wash the tears of sorrow.
Do not reveal the binding secret.

The park is almost empty,
it's at peace with the green-yellow birds,
the mellow sun sheds colour all around us, we say
nothing and look away for a precious moment.

Words will now melt bit by bit
through the spreading light, in our open palms,
not to forget our dreams
of the unending, eternal love.

# Draw Lines

See those scarred faces...empty eyes
Walking on the tightropes,
They stuck as if on a precipice...

Groped, ordered around and to the brink of disgust...
Stumble, fall down in fatigue but still
Laugh a little and sing the song of their lives...

Day in, tune on, day out, tune off,
They slug; hand work faster than loud mouth,
They are remembered only for their failures.

Evening sun probes their mind,
Wound, pain, agony roll into dry tears
A crushing blow; the struggle continues.

They earn happiness; they have to, for survival
They thrive on the pavements, on the slums, on the
ghettos.
They are our lifeline.

We draw a line of hunger, we dictate, we conclude
They want to live, they want to buy freedom
It's their only way of living life.

# Baobab

You stand alone on the pavement for days, months, years
You fall down in storm, pounded thoroughly yet survived,
Dried out as if beaten severely; still bear flowers and fruit.
Myths and legends; circle the world, soak in long stories.
Hit on the wall, flung from the paradise upside down into earth,
Birds and bees feel safe; draw food and nectar from the showy flowers.
You are burnt and stripped like humans yet again come out
Form new bark, new leaves, new life, and new ways to carry on.
We summon courage, inspire and instil our passion to live long.
The enormous thick trunk, the tapering branches, the roots
Lay bare for nine months; store gallons of water to survive,
The tree of life struggle hard and teach us a lesson in adversity.
We connive, we conspire but you dispose by your sheer strength
Death like all of us comes from rotten inside and collapse,
Still we need you inside our heart, in our mountain of sorrow.

# In The Light Of Truth

*The dew of compassion is tear- Lord Byron.*

A candle standing tall on the floor
The circle of light ends in itself,
The palpable darkness...for what it is.

Burning smell suffocates,
Shadows get shorter with time
Before the night's eye.

Cobwebs at the corner of the wall
To be blown away by the dusty wind,
As if the flash fire sears face and neck.

Soon the vast inky black sky
Turns into royal blue, the break of dawn.
The candle-lit words ... split us in pieces.

I know you have turned me against the universe
My voice entangled, tears conquer the myth,
I have to face you in the light of truth.

# Ecstasy

In the cocoon of intimacy
you may weave the same magic, raise the spirits
in a suave chemistry,
I dream about it in every breath I take
when I go to sleep.

that's not the right moment to think
about the hungry people and pale faces
the story with terrible problems, the lost love
and the effect of dying as
they curse and slay each other.

our stars are so strong, each time
night unfolds the puffy cheeks
the connection in soul level,
hides the wound and suffering,
supporting this lighter life in ecstasy.

# Inklings

last night was of drummers-
perched on the summit the dark clouds,
never quite get to grip with,
time collapses into a cloudy morning.

looking at the window
I do not need veil,
a slight drizzle on the cascade of lawns
spoiling the carnivals of bulbuls and parrots

hot water bottle in my bed,
big room with mosaic floor
and stuff leopards' stich stories,
of canals overflowing with cerium

inklings of life in a canvas,
are now plucking music from the air,
slipping so well in my skin,
I do not have any control.

upwelling of white clouds,
reaches for something,
now reveal,
sunlight and raindrops integrate nothing

# Your Silence

buried under my palm
the broken letters, the words in blue ink
framed in an A-4 size paper,

altering craving and emotion,
open their wounds,
the round mirror senses those percepts
you don't see, I can tell you all those names.

sometimes, not often,
memory losing muscles,
flows from one room to another
masks the timeline, an irretrievable past.

you were there, under the
scorching sun- frozen
no, not you but your eyes- frozen in silence.

I don't know, possibly not,
how to proceed or retreat?
is there anything to know at all?

# Troika

**1.**
still you connect me
to give hope, lean sharp shadows
on the concrete wall,
you wait there, fighting against
the inexorable pull.

**2.**
a need to escape
from everything around me
blue black with shadow.

time stuck in reverse
our tears fall in butchers' palm
frozen in cold wind.

in pitch perfect night
blue flame still burns in my thoughts
words melt in the heat.

**3.**
autumn shades and tones
shadows smell the memories
spy film fantasy.

sitting on the edge
still look for the crescent moon
the mystery lingers.

over the window
leaves fall in a hurry
my winter sets in.

# Immersive

We fall silent
thin layers of air between us
alter the intensity.

the shape and colour
of the evening clouds
immersive,
of your hands,

lonely sky.
use the metaphor,
I count stars in random digits.

my hands are empty,
put my head on your hand
stay alive-

the yellow scarf,
the tilt of your head,
in your hair, the brown pin.

frozen in my thin retina.

imagine a world elsewhere
full of perplexity
broken wings flutter less often,
surrender to the trampled grass.

I can only read river in your eyes
light up in earthen lamps

# Emission

Not enough, not nearly enough
The lights will change in a moment
End of an overture.

Sitting in this corner
We reopen the wound
You assume, I can't speak.

Pouring rain, haunted trees,
That's what you love to ignore
There is more to it confine with sleepy lines

With you light always slant low.
Make the most of sunshine.

Perhaps the deep voice, perhaps not,
Remains the very essence,

You say, for a better day, we seek
A way of fighting back.

Through the edges of the window,
The wind pierces our soul.

Not just recycling
A sense of possibility  rips up the whole.

## Surreal Canvas

let us walk on the garden path
gradually detach from the surroundings,
the empty moments
go. from one world to another,
and if not, I guess, still be with you.

everything behind those wooden doors
is true, full and meaningful,
a short stroll away,
the moss that outgrown on the brick wall,
the window is wet with tears.

the gestures, the glances, the slanted looks
the conversation that can't be heard,
not knowing who descend
the concrete stairs in a mad rush
to greet the known and unknown people.

the dark lines under your eyes
is an undertow, surreal on canvas,
my wary eyes and hunched shoulders
still in search of a sweet home
life is better here; say hello and embrace.

# Holy City

tonight rain clouds
slow-jamming the rising moon.

colours are poison
colours spit venom.

leached away
from hungry skin and bone.

widows walking barefoot
childhood bleeds.

a silent procession in darkness
towards the bathing ghat.

feel it between words
of desire and sin.

to wash the colours
thrown in white sari.

surrender to the tides
till the river collapses

they don't know when
the colours turn into poison.

suffer and remain opaque
till the moon disappears

# Home Coming

the broken glass window
negotiates the folds of time,
indeed sky is falling
I lift my face.

a heap of dust touching me passing,
contests the scheming wrath
of someone not present here,
I am because of you.

as if past and the present exist all at once
turning layers of the time plane
occur in unison
in my home coming.

flower beds and fountains
and much of its interiors,
once unrivalled in depth and diversity,
now lack eye watering opulence.

the old staircase drops gossips and stories,
finding no comfort here,
my silent calls echo down
the empty rooms and the courtyard
fill with layers of memories.

# Our Winter

Again I return to this room, shivering
in blistery wind, close the glass window,

our memory will outlast or perhaps
ought to be in the closet, the smell of

coffee triggers the salacious gossip and rumor
what keeps us burning right through,

A dim sky outside spending its own
reserves, cannot alter the course of history.

now the frosty wings lay bare the soul
and result in a chilling apocalyptic tale,

of snowflakes tuck in the black hair
even the low flame of the candle turns

its back. Even we repeat our sad song
fading slowly when we sit too close

facing the trials of foliage. Whisper
the code messages of the next winter.

# Walking On Alphabets

For now, morning sun unmasks the scarred face
It's just a jpeg image,
I am still here, the little bird tweets
on my laptops
behind the glass.

simmering beneath the unflappable exterior
eyes blazing with intensity
seen nerveless afternoon,
the possibility of visiting carnage
barely suppressed.

Now and then it happens
inside the ultra-thin arteries
feel the warmth
where colour used to pull the roses
and washes the cloudy rays.

walking on alphabets
the words survey,
the needle of a morphine syringe,
the distance to the deep shadows
of the X-ray films
where tossed up stars can't reach in a motion.

still waiting for the steely resolve
torching the dark cells,
filled with the song-
calling all crowd pullers,
and light up the steps to the Heaven.

## Spiral Leaf

In this vast land
to explore it a little further
for a moment, then not,
You have turned me into a spiral leaf

Pen and ink illustrations,
Watch me floating in the evening breeze
making sense for seeing through,
over stag and hen party animals.

Each birdsong is a letter to us
rise and scatter,
against me,
enter the moonlight, the haunted trees,
flapping wings, they all gone.

it does not matter what you will,
if the old magic read our quatrain,

in the heat of summer,
We drink a glass of dew water
and vanishes into the dark world.

Now that stars speak a dialect
no small thing to achieve,
sketching the dark hallow,
erasing dawn's sharp edge,

We knock the door of the blue sky.

# Solitary Confinement

We want to exit
and just go somewhere,
Just as heroic
This morning sun
Draws with a different brush.

In a solitary confinement
As often as you do
Rake the leaves, shovel the dust
Behind the thick bushes,
Clear away the path.

Your voice half-fills the room
Along one wall is a series of paintings,
Some sections of a branch
Overhang the low roof,
You want a new home.

A shadow reduces itself
To the edge of the narrow wall
That refracts light rays,
Steam rises from the floor
A summer evening comes to a halt.

# First Time

that was the first time you
decided to come with me,
not allowing me to regain my
consciousness.

I was not beautiful, you said before
tapping your fingers unmindfully,
unlacing your shoes as if disclosing
a high-stake secret.

a suave gentleman, you pretended
with your people pleasing eyes,
you knew that truth could always be
peeled into the petals of lies;

cross-stitching on my dress or
brush colours on the canvas,
the way rising plants resisted fingers,
I could refill my heart in my distress.

I could not fathom but stood silent
after receiving the phone call,
dark all the way.

still I could remember
what it meant to be starved.
forced it back where it was
I could find that little space,
for my strength, for my longing,
not easy to forget my hidden dreams.

# Tiny Raindrops

In my ancestral home
Winter took a hasty retreat
Summer was unnoticed
But those tiny raindrops showered inside.

We were not tamed
Sat on the elevated platform,
Laterite soil elsewhere in the shape
Of a mound, we were holding arms then
Under the leafy Arjun tree.

Conch shell blown, to the tune of
The evening serenade,
The bass notes filled with birds,
The creased bedcover, I could feel you.

Alone or together, the playful rehearsals
With you and I remembered the unknown
We didn't see there, but it was there,
Opened hidden wounds,
We could settle down to talk.

The shifting of light rays, the light that went out,
We saw it took shape, then fade away,
The last of the light, along the edge
Over the wooden slope, in a whispering note.

It was rousing, if only partially,
The old allegiance, never broke apart, never changing
Into anything else,

A story we knew later,
But not experienced.

# Salvation

And now more treats in store-

despite all its fancy entrance,
the snapping blinds,
its overload of details,
in the geometry of the lattice window,
are as if in convulsive seizures.

the pethidine induced rays of
the curved moon
soaking the narrow backstreet,
linger on the blue-green curtains
at the wooden door.

so it must have been
the edgy light washes
of the clammy skin
Or oddly turn down
towards the shuffling shadows.

and through the hue of scarcity
the prayers of breath, easy, intimate,
whisper into the ears
of the lonely widows
in deep places of their heart.

let the slothful night achieves freedom.

# Endless Whispers

Somewhere in the earth
the evening breeze
with tuft of feathers,
with birdsong
mention you.

the tenor in the voice of
the priest
at the distant temple,
the knowing that is
endless whispers.

for washing away
the deeply wound
igniting the silent moment,
in the rubble of life
of long prayers.

reach out to trees
the wind of the cold heights
destroys the cages,
connecting the light and shade
under open skies.

## Magic Spell


All those burning sticks
I want to throw back
on the dusty picture at the corner
of the room.

where everything is pieced together
in the arbitrary geometry of the shadow,
with a sense of small moments
preserved in between,

creating a new way of making
my faint memory alive.
not forgetting the
dust of yours and mine.

dancing on the rooftops,
to understand and find
at a moment's notice
that remembers what it means

to reinvent and exploit
the magic spells within
the cotton wool of love,
soaks in the mist of cold morning,
knots and in folded wings.

# Unhurried Music

We do not know where it ends.

At home we never talk about hungry tides and footprints
perhaps a reason,
that keeps us burning,

Because it makes sense,
We always float like a summer leaf before the dry winds.

The shining stars with their messy speeds
and energy
look for a hint of a curved moon

Walking on a trinket shop
We never wait to get upstairs to sing a love song.

Now the light of the orange vapor lamp hit
the water of the narrow canal.
we know what it means to be resting on each other.

For a moment between the two eager souls
echoes from a fort wall
break into tiniest pieces,

And evoke a sense of unhurried music.

# Sundeck

In that sundeck we were there reading the blue sky
and the sun flooded the sea front, the rugged cliff.

There was no sound of slamming of iron, no
painting of sunken eyes at the edge of the wall.

The rose petals dipped in water, stuck out
their dialects, here the wind was tight lipped,

Our low voice, we listened to something we have
heard before, words probably landed inside,

We put them back on the basket, the fresh
flowers, came out of their wet stillness,

A sketch book study on storm's eye, once
entertained us, one way you would feel,

Soft sigh perhaps, the swath of slow clouds
rubbing the skin, just hovered, asking for more.

A silence we absorbed at the surface, coming from
the south, erasing the deadly insomnia epidemic,

The lips awaken, from one bed to another
the kisses in resonance, lemon juice memories stayed
live.

# What People Are Saying

The secret code of Lahiri's poetry is his simple language of his own which is unique. His poems have simple titles and strength which communicate complex themes— Vihang Nayak [Gujrat]

Beautifully composed words leap effortlessly from Lahiri's pen. Poems in *Tidal Interlude* are precise, intense and critically self-conscious which radiate fresh rays from a glowing mind. The value that these poems give us is colorful paint to life and sensations of a man — Jaydeep Sarangi [Calcutta]

Lahiri's imagery is extraordinary, always invoking contrasts such as dark and light. Never far from his mind is the world of nature which is exalted in his poems. As many great poets do he sees himself both as part of nature and nature part of him inseparably — Rob Harle [Nimbin, Australia]

Gopal's master pen shows through as we take every step, watch every person, and hear every sound as we travel beside him — David J Delaney [Australia]

Lahiri's love of Nature continues unabated with hundreds of references to the Natural world. He refuses to see Nature as distinct from society; in fact he can't conceive of a human existence separate from it. And not just as mere adornment, the world of Nature exerts a necessary and positive influence – Gary Robinson [Canada]

Lahiri writes subtly, touching his thoughts with silk gloves yet leaves his finger prints like a painter's signature on his canvas. In many poems, he broods with a velvety mask creating a halo of sad romance but leaving a reader baffled if the poet is grieving or is happily drunk with his loss— Prabhanjan K Mishra [Mumbai]

Lahiri's genius lies in the use of words for analogies, only to make the reader to introspect and brood like himself indulgently and aesthetically — Seshu Chamarty [Hyderabad]